The Heart of Autumn

I0164397

Sable Quill Creations
http://www.sablequillcreations.com

N.L. Riviezzo

The Heart of Autumn
N.L. Riviezzo

Sable Quill Creations LLC
Manuscript Editing & Publishing Services
PO Box 4
Dacono, CO 80514
www.sablequillcreations.com

First Printing: September, 2011.
Printed in the United States of America

ISBN: 9780615523095

Cover Design by N.L. Riviezzo
Maple Leaves © Jaroslaw Grudzinski | Dreamstime.com

Dedication

For the one who is there
In the darkest moments
Even if she never truly understands

Table of Contents

Red and Gold – Part Four

Bleeding Indian Ink – Part Five

The
Heart
of
Autumn

Autumn

Fire-driven sorrow
Cascades gently down
Heart's ruins - a guise

Dead maple leaves
Festooned onto Death's hand
As she turns the card
Displaying a Cheshire grin
Expose pierian sins to
Coming winter dreams

Reason for celebration
Leaves shatter under
Footfalls swaying, stepping
In time to mental melodies

A change, a change
Maybe worse, maybe better
Only the ink decides

Decorating red and gold
Shard, discarded
Home found here
Celebrate in Death's
Autumn gown

Where life dwells
In disgraced ruins
Shut away by
A heart that bleeds
Indian Ink

Pierian Sins

Part One

On the Edge

Standing on the edge
Between light and dark
Heaven or hell
Some approximation of such places
A ripping chasm in the serenity
Water slipping through the cracks
Pull the chasm further apart
The sound creating thirst
Only an illusion if thought upon
Give the chasm consideration
And it will open its teeth
Chew until all has
Gone its way to fuel
Expansion increasing the
Dark fires burning
Along the paper-torn edges
Take these flames and smother
Smolder the traces and
Sprinkle out for the
Light to feast

Visions

Too far gone
In a world all
Alone nothing there
To love like the
Dreams wanted so badly
Made the disgust very
Clear, a retreat
Was issued to the
Comfort for the world
Inside all alone with
Imagination trying to make
It better assembling visions
Of hope to make
Life in the outer
World worth living when
Nothing cared - no
One could hear the tears
Breaking like a waterfall
Against their ears
Child gone to this realm
Eaten up by the heaping
Hate upon their shoulders
Only dreams could
Ease the burden
Now years have passed
And dreams break apart
As the outer world
Munches on them
Only the inner world is
Safe but the others are
Slowly creeping in
To set it ablaze

Cannibalistic Stances

When eyes close to dream
All that is seen are images
Driven by words read in
Past hours, days that
Cannot go away - lingering
Behind sight and thought
Making the skin crawl,
Twitch in disgust

Wanting it to past through
Make the dreams twist back
Some resemblance of the
Darkness they once bled
Into a strand of hope
Braiding and blocking
Out the disillusioned lights

Tried to lose the words
In strings of music
Among other thoughts
Visions of my own
Grabbed tighter to their
Cannibalistic stances
Growling, wanting undivided
Attention through slumber

Wake up, wake up
Carve the images out
Spit them up - ignore
The words once read
Bury them deeper down

Physical Form

Rarely ever here
Firmly planted to the ground
Floating above the physical plane
Tethered to the world by the
Crawling pain in heat
Leaving trails of cold sweat

The pain digs and digs
Skull and eyes scream

Wanting something tangible
Left with foggy sensations of
What should be, never is
No sense in crying

Go through the motions
Walking, talking, working
Hope no one notices that
The driver is missing from
View behind sleepy eyes

Pain dragging the physical form
Under invisible waters, drowning
Burning, suffocating life

So much missing, no claims
To be made on the past

Hope the night's dreams
Shove the beast out of spine
And bring new light to day

Haze

Struggling to find a way
A way through the haze
The brick wall of exhaustion
Hinder every aspect of waking hours
Of the thoughts and pen
The vice of caffeine
Despite major addiction
Helps so insufficiently
A true disappointment
Tasty but useless
Want to just sleep
Sleep it all away and hope
Tomorrow is better

A lie

A lie I tell myself
To think there is more
More to my life
Every day laced tightly
With caffeine wanting to
Keep exhaustion at bay
To let words flow freely
Most days fail miserably
Exhaustion — too formidable
A foe

Catalyst

Witnessing the precipice of
Your clear waters
Tearing us apart
Leaving quaking canyons
In the wake of these
Violations onto the earth

Held in my hands
Held in little colored glass jars
Lined up and waiting for
You to notice something more
Than yourself and your flowing power
Flowing out from under you
Only the earth can hold

Deny the earth and weave
Destruction in a musical
Methodical dance across
My heart crumbling away
And down the sides of canyons
Drawn across my back
Carved with your verbal blades
Flowing from your bloodied lips
Without care even when you
Land face down beneath
My feet

Coastlines

Weighed down by all
Those white powdered locks
And keys
Trying to cut them off
Unsuccessful as I
Sink into the voices
Unheard

Wondering if the path laid
Along the coast of
Ink and blood is the
Path I should take
To answer all these
Questions and find
Peace — pieces of
G-d hidden in the
Folds of night

Dig deep, dig down
To try, find everything
Anything worth clinging to
In the end
Am I even worthy of
Such a task at hand
What if the sea of
Ink and blood I created
In distress, too
High against its banks
Threatening to overflow
And kill me everything
I've tired to hold dear

Hit in downbeat
To teach me a lesson
As the waves crest against

The banks to taunt me
Knowing all my secrets
And all my sins I've
Tried to drown one
Too many times

Sins eroding those future
Dreams that seem
Overly contingent on their
Disappearance but it
Shouldn't be should I not
Grow and learn from them
To be a better person
Why can't I grow
Only flounder and flop along
Those white powdered banks

Choking, suffocating, viewing
My ink and blood
Floating by

Bad Medicine

Can it not be seen
These whispers of things come
And gone in a twirl
Bad medicine for my soul

As if I am assured
Got to find a way out
Suffocated and pulled in
Little vines dancing on singsong breezes
Bad medicine driven through

As if I am cured
Got to find balance
Before I tumble into myself
Left crying at my knees
Scarred and blackened
Bad medicine left to drift

As if I am assured
Got to find passion
Bound and fit to die

Heart Lies

Break my heart again
So many fissures
How was it even whole
To begin with
Eat up each piece
Not even stopping to relish
The taste of tears and
Soul fragments left behind

I try to be still
Not squirm or cry out under
The claws digging in
Skewering the sections left
Inside my bleeding chest
Breathe again and watch the
Blood spurt out to the
Rhythm of my lungs

Finish, finish the task
Take everything
Begging on my mental knees
For my savior
My redemption to take me home

Home, forgotten such a place
Home is not where my
Heart lies, lying in
Devoured tortured pieces
In the stomach of an abyss
Nowhere to go, only away
From flesh and bone

Uphill

Fighting uphill battles have never
Never been my specialty yet at every turn
It is there, that horrid hill in life
Always at the bottom looking up

Impossible things await
Traps with every pace
Look and tears well in
Eyes and soul looking up
Never looking down
Always down and wanting more

The underbrush digging into
My naked heels keeping me still
Trying to force me to move
Falter for humor's sake

Fighting and fighting
Only fighting phantoms of
Dreams that cannot be conquered
Until I reach the summit
Summit never in sight hidden
Among the thorns like trees
Playing shadows along the hillside

Run, run in taunt only still
Waiting, waiting for nothing
Looking up the hillside
Seeing nothing but the bloody tracks
I left behind as I tumbled back down
Down to the valley of my despair

Winter Dreams

Part Two

Noire

Fog settles like a dancer
Over one less shotgun morning
Seeking evil smiles to chill
With harsh embattled caresses
Over and over
While days stretch on
Breaking yellowed plaster
Mumble forbidden prayers in
Pillows ripping against claws
From dreams noire soaking
Bleach along rivers flooding
Blue blood swirls into a purple
Glaze add to a silver
Blade say that love
Is only the beginning
To the evil blossoming
Behind those purple eyes
Reflecting serene death along
A silver blade clutched in
Cracking fingers fall quicker
Plaster fall so a daggered
Death cannot bring this love
To tell and let it all in
Over and over again

Pristine

Want more, so much more
Like an addict down on
Their knees begging for a
Fix to everything that ails them
All an illusion - so perfectly
Sweet waiting for you
Blinded by the beauty
Get on your knees and
Pray that it see you
Grants wishes lurking in
Dreams and shrouded faith
Never felt love like this
So strong it burns flesh clean
From bones white, pristine

Sentinels

Ascend to the darkest night
No fears wait within
Find paths missing, overgrown
By neglect and shadow
Not ask of madness for reason
Even with answers splayed out
On mossy rocks, standing watch
Smelly sentinels to silent proceedings
Ascend into twilight
Waiting on the other side
Impatient and fickle, know not
Of day or night
Grey, black or white
Just to continue life
To the right of twinkling stars
Eyes on blue-black tapestry
Holding ascension in their tiny hands
Hands clutching, clutching
Trying so hard not to let go
Diminish into shadow

Midnight Sun

Wandering under the midnight sun
With the sparkling, weeping stars
Lusting after the one
Unattainable, a toxin
Wrong but longing lust cannot understand
Their weaknesses are only mine
Only the lust in passing
Midnight sun sees all the rejection
Laughing and mocking
While the stars cry
Cry in humor-driven sympathy

Nowhere Home

Filled with the dust
Of good intentions
Filed in and away
Hopes lost in covered light
Little twinges under skin
Crawling up and down
Unrivaled eulogies
Stagnated by the lead
Of disgraced ink
Stark dreams asphyxiated
By this false guise
Days under warrant
Gathering of flowers
In ashes to hide
The hollow, dug out
From once good
Intentions

Forgotten Starlight

Tether down this uproar
Rip it apart like feathers
To see if it can be put
Together in a fashion
That makes sense of it all
Knowing not what makes
It tick and function through the
Everyday is exhausting
Who wants such trial
And error day in, day
Out and over again
"Not I!" exclaimed these
Eyes of blue-green ocean tide
Wading deeper and deeper
Into the internal bliss
Of not seeking the pandemonium
But of the mayhem finding
A way to dig at the porcelain
Underground cracking, breeding
Affirmations of forgotten starlight
Lost in silhouetted veils

Snow

This Mayfair mistress held
Hostage by the snow
Driven with meager intentions
Have no reason to cry tears
They'll be your everything
Stumbling over drifts of
Massacred flesh lost
At sea set afire
For what you'll never do
Roped up around the neck
Dangling waiting to be
Broken down as you
Stumble and fake it
With false destinies
Set your heart alight
And hold on to the
Melting snow

Lacking

You sway to my siren song
As if you know me
Yet I am the perpetual
Enigma so you will never
Know me or the song
Within my heart
You crave to know
And are slighted when
Proof to the contrary
Is presented clearly
In my actions, movements
Step away and stop seeking
I will not share with you
For you lack the proper
Rhythm to truly comprehend
What drives what moves
Me in my life
Unworthy, just walk away
As I cannot abide you

Dark Wishes

Amethyst dreams that create
A falling sky as thoughts
Merge in borderline skate
Skating on the edge
Wanting a peaceful but never
Scenic scene that they can
Hold for all eternity
Eluding them this want
Skating, dancing
An imaginary tango
Thoughts and hope coming together
With sensuality that smokes
A darkened wish into mist
Fleeting, floating and dancing
Dancing away on a breeze
To broken amethyst dreams

Deeply

Echoes sweep from lips as
They distort against agony
Lit up across skylines

Pay no attention to silent
Explosions locked in spines

Twisting, grinding while
Demise loves them deeply

Too deeply for even shadows
Lights blind then shielded
By grey velvet for mere
Bittersweet moments

Pull, pull the velvet away
Rip it to pieces with
A frenetic vigor unmatched

Cling to the tattered grey and
Cry – no journey has ever
Hurt like this fury

Fingers tightly clinched around
Fading grey clouds demanding to
Reunite with their poisons

Floating away, never easing
Unspeakable pain that still
Holds, twists and tears out
Any ounce of unquenched introverted
Humanity lingering in grey wisps

Clouding crying eyes, protecting
The soul from truths only

Night whispers in veins

Mental Melodies

Part Three

She Brings

She brings out the secrets in others
Sees the secrets trying
Trying so desperate to hide
So much hate for her
Afraid that she will spill
Spill more than blood
When the day is said and done

She brings out the worst in others
Brings those skeletons out
To parade across her face
Strip her down and make the world a mess for her
Leave her black, blue and crimson
Shatter her so she no longer knows
Who she is, torn between the reality
And the visions she clings to
To hide from the monsters lingering under
Illusions of serene flesh

She brings out the worst in others
Brings out the worst in herself
As she cries out on bended splintered knees
In her mind's eye
A mind fragmented, scrambling to cope
Scrambling to find a mask
That will make everything seem peaceful
The calm ocean surface
Hiding the death awaiting within
Much like those who leave her broken
Taking much more than their lies
From what she is

The tattoos of pain dancing
Across her torn skin
Torn in the agony of piecing her mind

Piecing her mind together again
Preparing it for another attack from enemies
She cannot see and see absolute
Bracing for another arrow of words for her heart
Another fist to find placement on her body
Always finding their targets perfectly

She brings out the hate in others
So she hates herself, punishes herself
For shortcomings she cannot unravel
Making her flesh bleed
Bleed out their words ripping her up
Ripping from the inside out
Seeping the hate out in little rivers
Rivers marking tracts along the scars
Little pain pictures for her to relish
If she could only remember how
How the marks got there

She brings out the violence in others
Only to wear it for herself
A testament to the evil she
Holds within that wants
To feel, feel the pain
Pain she can never tolerate
But cannot get enough of
So they strip her down and make
Her world a mess to sift through
Her fingers as she cries, bleeds
Making the clay to build anew

She brings out herself in others

Intrigues

She came in hopes
The sentinels would show mercy
Grant her long buried desires

Little child's fantasies
She whispers as she sinks
Tapered under the dark blue
Lapping at her bound form

She came to this place
Mirage of opulence
In hopes everything would
Would find peace and place

Betrayed so sweetly
By warm kisses
Given by a stoic man
Who wanted for not
Born into absolute luxury

She - a mere pawn in
His intrigues
She too blinded by gold
To see the Reaper
Lurking about in her wake

A little dance, a little sway
Around every bend and thought

Her dark curls float above
Spread out among the descending waves
Marking her fitful passage

Grey towers watch on
Bricks marred by sunset

Shadows descend as she slips
Slips further into the deep

Breach

Come within reach
So I may squish – squish you
As it is meant to be
Little evil things you do
Tormenting me tormentingly
Waiting, watching, wandering
Never knowing where you'll be

Come within reach
Meet death by my hand
Promise it will not hurt
But for a second, no longer
No need to fear
For you do not belong here
With me, within this space

Violated the treaty granting
Death to you quick and simple
Not playing by the rules
Running, taunting
Death so close, so far

Come within reach
Ease the breach of contract
Be absolved of your sins
Greet death by my hand
Promise it will not hurt
But for a second, no longer

Heartrending

Words missing true sincerity
Yet they escape out into the open
Making others cry along
With false melancholy that the
Words traveled with in a
Carefully crafted farce
Hollow, empty even behind
The eyes from which the tears
Did flow once upon a time
They may have meant something
But now just a joke with
A choke hold on the future
And present struggling
To drag down even more
Emotions to devour feeding
The deceptions

Fail

Mental images fail like seasons
Around written feet, stomping out
The fires, words fail to
Create talk to the page
But it does not listen
It fails to see what the
Heart wants to express
So outnumbered and still
Images fall forth never
Knowing any better
Sweep them up, the
Little broken buts
Try to glue them to
A page to make sense
Failing and failing
Light them on
Fire and hope the
Smoke and flames make
More of an impression on
The sky than they do
On the earth

The Liars' Waltz

What lies should I say
To keep you near to torment

What lies are you going to
Utter to force me to believe
To keep me from pushing you
Away

Forever in this little game
Just wanting to hurt each other
Because you're nothing without
Me

Because I'm not everything I
Hoped and you love it

Licking one another's wounds
In a pained embraced
One more time
One more miniature deceit
To make it go down more
Smoothly

Every scream in the night
Delights your agenda
Peeling off my soul
Like little stickers that
Form a picture on the side
Of the asylum where you reside

Wanting to be alive outside of
These lies but where would
That leave us at the end of the
Day and night
As I sin over and over again

In spite of you

My heart knows not of
Your warmth, the peace you claim
To possess

I find only agony in your arms
Twisting and turning
Betwixt and between, I find
Us once more at this crossroads
Constantly coming here to battle it
Out yet coming up empty

An emptiness increasing my contempt
For every whisper, lie, false hope
You keep in the folds of words
Long written, long forgotten
But still deadly in this world

All because you can't just
Let it go

Holding the Trigger

Claws running down the back
Looking for the trigger among
Earthquakes of the soul
Never give it away
Feel the soul burning the trigger alive
But it is here feeling the claws
Never seeing them, the pain
Leaves traces in the beauty
It can't need anything yet it
Begs for the cold comfort of
Your heart
Will you be its martyr as the
Trigger swallows you whole
The earthquakes rattle on with
The claws digging deeper and deeper
Wrapping around the neck
Wanting to snap it in half, making
The pale flesh run cold

Floodwater

Tears tear at the levees
Of the heart

Tears break it all apart
No matter the cause or
Means of prevention
Emotional flood will overtake
This body

Letting the self turn to
Water cascading out
Such force to hold back
Brings agony beyond belief

Tear the tears
Hold them near
Fashion a little patch
Try to ease the burdened levees
Learn to select the leaks
Eradicating a complete flood

Only streams of emotional distress
Perforate the levees

Child's Eyes

Sweet child
Do not cry
Dry your amethyst eyes
Days come and go in a
Mysterious tango
Hang on tight
Try not to fall
Over the borderline
Dividing days from
Nights of disparity
Away from the scenic and peaceful
World you should know
Leaving naughty footprints
In its wake
Drag you down
Drag you up
A never ending game
This tango of living

Freedom in Breath

Bring out the worse
Then it gets taken out on me
Know every angle of the deceit
As they crumble down
Down to my ankles
Crushing under bare feet - hemorrhaging
Along jagged edges

Means so little
To the pain coming
Come from the form
Building up, festering
Waiting to push me
Push me to my knees
Beseech

Beseeching for mercies that
Will never find sound or notice
Locked with visions
Visions of monsters only seen
From my perch upon the knees
Crusted in crimson facade
Tattooing the skin
Reminding me - only me
Of those I come to witness
In truth

Strip me down, know my
World as strikes fly
Bringing me to the ground
As the monster behind heart
Finds freedom in my breath

Red and Gold

Part Four

The Undertaker

Fingers drawing the outlines
Of your tattoos covering
Every inch of skin
Malicious or funny
Depending on your mood
In the early morning hours
Before fear and intimidation
Rip us apart - only in the
Moments like these does
Love exist between us
Secrets and your murderous
Intentions making what we are
Come apart at the
Seams for the sun and
Twilight to see
Bury it all down with
Your enemies, the corpses
Left in your wake
Then come back to be
Between my arms, my thighs
Leaving the outside world behind

Rapture

Dreamed of Death again
Came to drag his
Suggestive fingers across
My pulse quickening
Longing and hungry
Both fighting deprivation
Wanting me to
      Live

Long enough to be of
Purpose to his needs
Fighting the means of
      Being

Everything he stands for
Take me in rapture
I do not fear you
Taste me
Make me feel again
Make me feel anything but
      Empty

All worth the while
The erratic pulse dancing
Singing out such a
Lovely little melody to
Tempt Death's hunger

Trail of Blood

Taking the body down
Starting the mourning process
Praying for the rebirth of a
Violently taken soul with
Vacant eyes and empty veins

Drained in a fit of passion
Words of remorse explode
Against empty walls seeing everything
So much regret for one
Corpse to hold even in
Death as the flesh runs
Cold along the fireplace at
Its feet

Come back to
Me

Blood trickling
And choking every cry
Mistakes, so many mistakes

All for a love that will
Wilt like roses in winter
But it no longer means
Anything to the corpse
At its lover's bended knees
Dripping forth bloody tears
For the departed -

Come forth to the night
Beautiful wilted rose, winter
Should not have come for
You, please return
Return to me

Holding Casanova

Line up the tracks
Trying to forget the
Poison of your lips
Left on the laces
Of my dress as
I waited to be
Unbound and given
Leave to this reality for
A world belonging to us
And us alone
Still standing with this craving
But enraged at the mistake –
Believing your precious
Careful words making me
Weak at the knees
Sweet little Casanova locking
Me in with your carefully
Woven words of romantic
Interludes that I can only
Dream about, wish for
Making my cell out of shattered
Wishes and dreams keeping me
Inside never to be played with
Only sit in the ever piling anger
Trying desperately to pick the
Lock so I can devour you and
Keep you always

Aspect of Mourning

Mourning's last delicate graces
Are defiled against the smile
Twisted across your snow-tinted
Face in the dead of night

Stars flee in the promise of
Necromancy under this new moon
Brought about consumed innocence
Twist it all around further and further
Till the binds break in splinters

Grace falls to its knees in penance
For nothing can fix its folly
Siding with the beautiful visage
That Death bears means
Only the end for its intentions
For all things unholy and impure

Upon this earth, swallow grace whole
Mourning drops her bonnet at the grave
From which Death rose at the clanging
Of the Midnight hour in search
Longing for blood – plain,
Simple, the eternal essence

Campfire

A simple caress
That is missed
Delicate sweet
Erotic and discreet
Behind the backdrop
Of flames
A private moment
That one has no
Longer, only to watch
And want from a
Distance
A simple caress
Lips upon hands
Delicate sweet
Erotic and meant
For another

Tiny Heart

Choose and choose wisely
This moment will pass by
In the blink of an eye
This shadow will not come
By again to claim

Make a choice for more
More than what this tiny heart
Can be in the night
In this blood

Tiny wise heart so forced
To a day that it cannot be
Part of no matter how
Hard it tries

Crying tiny heart
Trapped in depression further
Locked down by the happiness
Of others surrounding the bleeding
Shell of a girl wearing her mask
Of disgusting makeup

Tiny heart on its knees
Waiting for the answers

Waiting

May You...

May you lose your footing
Just like I did so many
Years ago in my heart

May you know the
Faint death of forgiveness
Like a sweet breeze
Upon scarred and scared
Lips that never bestow
Kisses in this time

May you know the knife
Of repented sins never
Granted by what you
Hold holy and unholy

May you feel the pain
That the word 'never' brings
While trying to sweep it
All under the rug in vain

May your words be captured
In disbelief by everyone
You cross paths with
For they will see you
As the wolf in woolen fleece

Beautiful Twilight

I sit here licking my wounds
Time and time again because
Of what you do to me
But I like the taste so I refuse
To give up, give in

In this dark little corner
I exclaim your name in
Shunned prayer against
The music of my heart
I know nothing of what I say
What I hear, what I smell
For I have forgotten
The importance of the senses

I never paid attention to them
In the beginning – why start now
I only acknowledge the pain
Foreign unhinged beautiful
Twisted up in my demented variations
Of what pleasure should be
Of what drives my caged libido
Locked up in youth still fighting
To have a chance to prove

Its rights against what claws
Up the flesh and leaves me
Lapping up my own blood
From fine porcelain
Just like a cat in the twilight

En Avant

Know this dancer twirling around
Trying to run from what this life
Has given her but it's so hard
To avoid

Everything brings a passion
That's hard to ignore
Wanting to cling to the art
But needing to drill it out
Of her skull

The visions and the recaps
Cast shadows over the dance floor
As she twists and turns displaying
A quaint madness to this
Audience of silence
It is never really over
For her

Always dancing for her life
Relishing in each second
Each movement, each turn
All have meanings tied to
A moment experienced
In love, in the ordinary

Tears can't fall from
Those eyes as she's not
Real, just a figment
Of the conscience mind
That can never truly encapsulate
The world it experiences in prose

So the dancer keeps dancing
Hoping to dye her dress in the

Ink of the soul that she cycles
Through in every *fouetté* and *plié*

Bleeding Indian Ink

Part Five

I Write...

I write because words torment
In night, in sleep
In breath, in dream
For love's contentment

I write for glimpses
Of sanity which cannot
Be held until they are
Trapped, sandwiched between
Paper and ink

I write to express worlds
Only imagined, to share
My joys and passions

I write for me to fill
Solitude and to find
Meaning in all things
Seen and unseen, holy and unholy

I write for words
Everything finds a way
To hold their lives in words
Like blood, words flow
Bringing nourishment and essence
A reason to live

I write because it is
My soul, etched out in
Beautiful words so lovely
On paper with luscious ink

Inked

Sacrificed my teen-aged angst
Over to inked pages
And scars on flesh
Still here and seemingly fine
Against withered hearts of
Licking time that pause
Along tacks laid out by
Ink, tears and razor blades
Call out to the pieces left
Behind inside each word formulating
A testament of affliction that
I could not imagine but
Were my burdens alone to
Bare with each passing day
Ink may fade yet memories always stay
Locked inside, the intents repeating
In my mind wanting more
Ink to ease the linger essences
Of the pain and the pain alone

Precious Plague

My precious plague
Of twisted dreams
Let me hear you
S
  C
    R
      E
        A
          M
Make me feel alive
Give me breath
Let me dwell in
Your fantasy

My precious plague
Of twisted dreams
Let me hear you
      T
    W
  I
  S
T
Make me feel depths
Give me thoughts
Let me dwell in
Your nightmares

My precious plague
Of twisted dreams
Let me hear you
B
  R
    E
      A
        K

-66-

Make me feel hollow
Give me darkness
Let me dwell in
Your inferno

Slumber

This room
I can feel it in
My dreams
Surrounded by books
Containing knowledge I cry out
For in the dark when dreams
Become nightmares I cannot
Escape from even with ink
By my side
They will linger like waves
Wavering, crashing, drowning
Killing me as I slumber against
Cotton covered pillows
Wanting more warmth as
The nights cool heralding a
New season is coming to play
Offering new inspirations and
New contagious fears to remark
On in my tears of desperation

Flawed Whole Perfect

Write it out, my child
Bring it to the light
Do not feel shame
For your words - you are
Flawed whole perfect
Things seem to be patterns
Ignore and just focus
Therapy for a battered soul
Write it out and find
Solace everything needed to feel
Feel again see colors once more
Know humanity know it
Holds on inside
A little spoiled yet usable
If you try hard enough to
Unburden the words

Gossamer

Write the words
Try to make them sing
Sweet, sweet songs
If they do not
It will not mean
A thing as to someone
They will be the
Most precious melody
Write the words
Think not of what they mean
As long as they keep with theme
The soul of the piece
Leeching through the ink
Infecting the reader
Emotions portrayed in sweet
Black ink songs giving
New life to which once was
Dead, dying, hanging on
By tiny gossamer threads
Write the words
Editing is a sin
Just write
Everything works out in the end

Yes of Simple Words

Add up simple words
Feeling overwhelmed
So many words to piece
Pieces are tiny things
Need to ensure more pieces
The outline is all wrong
Chose wrongly?
No, no

This is right
Suppose to be a challenge
Need to yield such results for
Ultimate success
Success to be earned
Brutally with ink smudged fingers
Take it all in stride
Stride over paper to make
Something of one's self
Yes, yes

Effort to be greatly rewarded
By accomplishment
By more paper
Paper, white and green
Or so says dreams
Sweet little things
Those colorful dreams
But will they come true
If worlds succeed in
Finding life on this paper
Coated in thoughtful words

Remind Me

These words scream out
Into your soul trying
To kill you in remembrance
Of the person I truly am
Writing out my thoughts onto
Paper daggers bloodied
Such sullied intentions locked
Into place push and
Pull nothing but agony to be
Felt and dug from the dirt
Caked against downtrodden feet
Remind me, remind me again
Why should I open ears to
Your fool's prattling when emptiness
Seems to be unchanged except the spikes
Driven into your feet on a
Nightly basis looking through the
Bottom of a bottle to mask
The pain as they travel downward

Little Ink Cradles

Pieces of me
Dying slowly under the heat
Of Indian Summer
Without words to shade and soothe

Need the words like oxygen
Come back to me
Come back
Need you too much
My heart, my soul, my life
All wrapped up in utterances
Tied together with an ink bow

Let me cradle you once more
Try so hard not to let go
Again I don't want to suffer
Not like this

Little precious words
Come back, please
Please, don't leave me to
Drown and die in agonizing sorrow
At your untimely departure

Taffy

Honesty is a fickle mistress
Often wrapped up in a cloak
A cloak of lies
Where does honesty dwell
Perhaps in the crevasses of soul-kin
All that is grasped is the illusion
Illusion of cloak drawn out,
stretched out into a beautiful array
A beautiful rainbow of lies
Little bits of bitter taffy
Sprinkled out crushed under footfalls
Trying to run, run from honesty
Never understanding that lies
Lies are all honesty had
Had to build upon

Acknowledgments

I would like to thank my mom for putting up with my artist moodiness over the years, Devin O'Branagan for her support with this project, the readers over at Devin's Forum for putting up with all my poetry pieces even when they had zero idea what to do with them and those who have taken time to read this book.

*****

About the Author

N.L. Riviezzo has been writing poetry for over fifteen years. Many of her works have won honorable mention in various poetry competitions and several others have been published in newspapers and magazines. *The Heart of Autumn* is her first full-length publication. When she is not busy writing poetry, she can be found reading, inventing recipes, sewing, recreating the Middle Ages, editing manuscripts and spending time with her three fur children. She lives in Colorado. Visit her at **www.words-scribbled.com**.